The Rosicrucian Hermetic

Romance Or Chymical Wedding

Rosicrucian Brothers

THIS ARTICLE WAS EXTRACTED FROM THE BOOK:

Mysteries of the Rosie Cross

BY THIS AUTHOR:

Rosicrucian Brothers

ISBN 1564596982

READ MORE ABOUT THE BOOK AT OUR WEB SITE:

http://www.kessinger.net

OR ORDER THE COMPLETE
BOOK FROM YOUR FAVORITE STORE

ISBN 1564596982

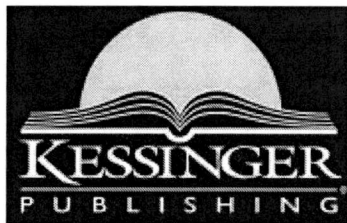

CHAPTER VII.

The Hermetick Romance ; or Chymical Wedding.

A REMARKABLE work was published at Strasbourg, in the year 1616, entitled, " The Hermetick Romance : or the Chymical Wedding. Written in High Dutch by Christian Rosencreutz." This book though not given out to the world until the above year, is said to have existed in manuscript for some time previously, as far back in fact as 1601, thus making it the oldest Rosicrucian book extant. A modern writer says : The whole Rosicrucian controversy centres in this publication, which Buhle describes as a comic romance of extraordinary talent.

Owing to its importance, we shall have to make some lengthy extracts from the translation made in 1690, by E. Foxcroft of King's College, Cambridge. It is arranged in chapters, denominated days, marked from one to seven.

The First Day.

On an evening before Easter Day, I sate at a Table, and having (as my custom was) in my humble prayer sufficiently conversed with my Creator, and considered many great mysteries (whereof the Father of Lights his Majesty had shewn me not a few) and being now ready to prepare in my heart, together with my dear Paschal Lamb, a small unleavened, undefiled cake ; all on a sudden ariseth so horrible a tempest, that I imagined no other but that through its mighty force, the hill whereon my little house was founded, would fly in pieces. But in as much as this, and the like from the devil (who had done me many a spite) was no new thing to me ; I took courage and persisted in my meditation, till somebody (after an unusual manner) touched me on the back ; whereupon I was so highly terrified, that I durst hardly look about me ; yet I shewed myself as cheerful as (in the like occurrences) human frailty would permit. Now the same thing still twitching me several times by the coat, I looked back, and behold it was a fair and glorious lady whose garments were all skye colour, and curiously (like Heaven) bespangled with golden stars. In her right hand she bare a trumpet of beaten gold, whereon a name was engraven (which I could well read in) but am as yet forbidden to reveal it. In her left hand she had a great bundle of letters of all languages, which she (as I afterwards understood) was to carry into all countries. She had also large and beautiful wings, full of eyes throughout, wherewith she could mount aloft and fly swifter than any eagle. I might perhaps have taken further notice of her, but because she staid so small a time with me, and terror and amasement still possessed me, I was fain to be content. For as soon as I turned about, she turned her letters over and over, and at length drew out a small one, which with great reverence she laid down upon the table, and without giving one word departed from me. But in her mounting upwards, she gave so mighty a blast on her gallant trumpet, that the whole hill echoed thereof, and for a full quarter of an hour after, I could hardly hear my own words.

In so unlooked-for an adventure, I was at loss, how either to advise or assist my poor self, and therefore fell upon my kness, and besought my Creator to permit nothing contrary to my eternal happiness to befall me ; whereupon with fear and trembling I went to the letter which was now so heavy, as had it been mere gold, it could hardly have been so weighty. Now as I was diligently viewing it, I found a little Seal, whereupon a curious cross with this inscription, IN HOC SIGNO VINCES, was engraven.

Now as soon as I espied this sign I was the more comforted, as not being ignorant that such a Seal was little acceptable, and much less useful to the Devil. Whereupon I tenderly opened the letter

and within it, in an Azure Field, in Golden Letters, found the following verses written—

> This day, this day, this, this
> The Royal wedding is.
>
> Art thou thereto by birth inclin'd
> And unto joy of God design'd,
> Then mayst thou to the mountain tend
> Whereon three stately Temples stand,
> And there see all from end to end.
>
> Keep watch and ward,
> Thyself regard ;
> Unless with diligence thou bathe,
> The Wedding can't thee harmless save :
> He'll damage have that here delays,
> Let him beware, too light that weighs.

Underneath stood Sponsus and Sponsa.

As soon as I had read this letter, I was presently like to have
fainted away, all my hair stood on end, and a cold sweat trickled
down my whole body.   For although I well perceived that this
was the appointed wedding, whereof seven years before I was ac-
quainted in a bodily vision, and which now so long time I had with
great earnestness attended, and which lastly, by the account and
calculation of the Planets, I had most diligently observed, I found
so to be, yet could I never foresee that it must happen under so
grievous and perilous conditions.   For whereas I before imagined
that to be a welcome and acceptable guest, I needed only be ready
to appear at the wedding; I was now directed to Divine Providence,
to which until this time I was never certain.   I also found by myself, the more I examined myself, that in my head there was nothing
but gross misunderstanding and blindness in mysterious things, so
that I was not able to comprehend even those things which lay
under my feet, and which I daily conversed with, much less that I

should be born to the searching out and understanding of the secrets of Nature ; since in my opinion Nature might everywhere find a more *vertuous* disciple, to whom to intrust her precious, though temporary and changeable treasures. I found also that my bodily behaviour, and outward good conversation, and brotherly love towards my neighbour, was not duly purged and cleansed ; moreover, the tickling of the flesh manifested itself, whose affection was bent only to pomp and bravery, and worldly pride, and not to the good of mankind ; and I was always contriving how by this art I might in short time abundantly increase my profit and advantage, rear up stately palaces, make myself an everlasting name in the world, and other the like carnal designs.   But the obscure words concerning the Three Temples did particularly afflict me, which I was not able to make out by any after speculation, and perhaps should not yet, had they not been wonderfully revealed to me.   Thus sticking betwixt hope and fear, examining myself again and again, and finding my own frailty and impotency, not being in any wise able to succour myself, and exceedingly amazed at the fore-mentioned threatening ; at length I betook myself to my usual and most secure course ; after I had finished my earnest and most fervent prayer, I laid me down in my bed, that so perchance my good angel by the Divine permission might appear, and (as it had formerly happened) instruct me in this doubtful affair, which to the praise of God, my own good, and my neighbour's hearty and faithful warning and amendment did now likewise fall out.   For I was scarce fallen asleep, when me-thought, I, together with a numberless multitude of men lay fettered with great chains in a dark dungeon, wherein, without the least glimpse of light, we swarmed like bees over one another, and thus rendered each other's affliction more grievous.   But although neither I, nor any of the rest could see one jot ; yet I continually heard one heaving himself above the other, when his chains or fetters were become ever so little lighter,

though none of us had much reason to shove up the other, since
we were all captive wretches.   Now as I with the rest had con-
tinued a good while in this affliction, and each was still reproaching the other with his blindness and captivity, at length we heard
many trumpets sounding together, and kettle-drums beating so
artificially thereto, that it even revived and rejoiced us in our
calamity.

During this noise, the cover of the dungeon was from above
lifted up, and a little light let down unto us.   Then first might
truly have been discerned the bustle we kept, for all went pesle-
mesle, and he who perchance had too much heaved up himself,
was forced down again under the others feet.   In brief, each one
strove to be uppermost, neither did I myself linger, but with my
weighty fetters slipped up from under the rest, and then heaved
myself upon a stone, which I laid hold of ; howbeit, I was several
times caught at by others, from whom yet as well as I might, with
hands and feet, I still guarded myself.   For we imagined no other
but that we should all be set at liberty, which yet fell out quite
otherwise.   For after the nobles, who looked upon us from above
through the hole, had a while recreated themselves with this our
struggling and lamenting, a certain hoary headed Ancient Man,
called to us to be quiet, and having scarce obtained it, began (as I
still remember) thus to say :—

> If wretched mankind would forbear
>   Themselves so to uphold,
> Then sure on them much good confer
>   My righteous mother would.
> But since the same will not insue
> They must in care and Sorrow rue,
>   And still in Prison lie.
> Howbeit my dear mother will
>   Their follies over-see,

Her choicest gifts permitting still
    Too much in th' Light to be.
Though very rarely it may seem
That they may still keep some esteem,
Which else would pass for forgery.
Wherefore in honour of the Feast
    We this day solemnize,
That so her Grace may be increast
    A good deed she'll devise,
For now a cord shall be let down,
And whosoe'er can hang thereon,
    Shall freely be releast.

He had scarce done speaking, when an ancient matron commanded her servants to let down the cord seven times into the dungeon, and draw up whosoever could hang upon it. Good God! that I could sufficiently describe the hurry and disquiet that then arose amongst us, for every one strove to get at the cord, and yet only hindered each other. But after seven minutes a sign was given by a little bell, whereupon at the first pull the servants drew up four. At that time I could not come near the cord by much, having to my huge misfortune, betaken myself to a stone at the wall of the dungeon, and thereby was disabled to get to the cord which descended in the middle. The cord was let down the second time, but divers because their chains were too heavy, and their hands too tender, could not keep their hold on the cord, but with themselves beat down many another, who else, perhaps, might have held fast enough; nay, many an one was forcibly pulled off by another who yet could not himself get at it; mutually envious were we even in this our great misery. But they of all others most moved my compassion whose weight was so heavy that they tore their very hands from their bodies, and yet could not get up. Thus it came to pass that at these five times, very few were drawn up. For as soon as the sign was given, the servants were so nimble at the draught, that the most part tumbled one upon another, and the cord, this time especially, was drawn up very empty. Whereupon the greatest part, and even I myself, despaired of Redemption, and called upon God that he would have pity on us, and (if possible) deliver us out of this obscurity, who also then heard some of us : for when the cord came down the sixth time, some of them hung themselves fast upon it, and whilst in the drawing up, the cord swung from one side to the other, it (perhaps by the will of God) came to me, which I suddenly catching, got uppermost above all the rest, and so at length beyond hope came out ; whereat I exceedingly rejoiced, so that I perceived not the wound, which in the drawing up I received on my head by a sharp stone, till I with the rest who were released (as was always before done) was fain to help at the seventh and last pull, at which time through straining, the blood ran down all over my clothes, which I nevertheless for joy regarded not. Now when the last draught whereon the most of all hung was finished, the matron caused the cord to be laid away and willed her aged son (at which I much wondered) to declare her resolution to the rest of the Prisoners, who after he had a little bethought himself, spoke thus unto them :

> Ye children dear,
> All present here,
> What is but now compleat and done,
> Was long before resolved on :
> What ev'r my mother of great grace
> To each on both sides here hath shewn
> May never miscontent misplace ;
> The joyful time is drawing on,
> When every one shall equal be,
> None wealthy, none in penury.

Who ev'r receiveth great commands,
Hath work enough to fill his hands.
Who ev'r with much hath trusted been,
'Tis well if he may save his skin.
Wherefore your lamentations cease,
What is't to waite for some few days.

As soon as he had finished the words, the cover was again put
and locked down, and the trumpet and kettle-drums began afresh,
yet could not the noise thereof be so loud but that the bitter
lamentation of the prisoners which arose in the dungeon was above
all, which soon also caused my eyes to run over. Presently after
the ancient matron, together with her son, sat down upon seats
before prepared, and commanded the Redeemed should be told.
Now as soon as she understood the number, and had written it
down in a gold-yellow tablet, she demanded every one's name,
which were also written down by a little page ; having viewed us
all, one after another, she sighed, and spoke to her son, so as I
could well hear her. 'Ah ! how heartily am I grieved for the poor
men in the dungeon ! I would to God, I durst release them all,'
whereunto her son replied ; ' It is, mother, thus ordained of God,
against whom we may not contend. In case we all of us were
lords, and possessed all the goods upon earth, and were seated at
table, who would there then be to bring up the service ?' whereupon
his mother held her peace, but soon after she said ; ' Well, however, let these be freed from their fetters,' which was likewise
presently done, and I, except a few, was the last, yet could I not
refrain, but (though I still looked upon the rest) bowed myself
before the ancient matron, and thanked God that through her, He
had graciously and fatherly vouchsafed to bring me out of such
darkness into the light : after me the rest did likewise, to the sa-
tisfaction of the matron. Lastly, to every one was given a piece of
gold for a remembrance, and to spend by the way, on the one side

whereof was stamped the rising sun, on the other (as I remember) these three letters, D. L. S., and therewith everyone had license to depart, and was sent to his own business, with this annexed intimation, that we to the glory of God should benefit our neighbours, and reserve in silence what we had been intrusted with, which we also promised to do, and so departed one from another. But in regard of the wounds which the fetters had caused me, I could not well go forward, but halted on both feet, which the matron presently espying, laughing at it, and calling me again to her, said thus to me, My son, let not this defect afflict thee, but call to mind thy infirmities, and therewith thank God who hath permitted thee even in this world, and in the state of thy imperfection to come into so high a light, and keep these wounds for my sake. Whereupon the trumpets began again to sound, which so affrighted me that I awoke, and then first perceived that it was only a dream, which yet was so strongly impressed upon my imagination, that I was still perpetually troubled about it, and methought I was yet sensible of the wounds on my feet. Howbeit, by all these things I well understood that God had vouchsafed that I should be present at this mysterious and hidden wedding; wherefore with child-like confidence I returned thanks to his Divine Majesty, and besought him that he would further preserve me in this fear, that he would daily fill my heart with wisdom and understanding, and at length graciously (without my desert) conduct me to the desired end. Hereupon I prepared myself for the way, put on my white linen coat, girded my loins with blood-red ribbon, bound crossways over my shoulder; in my hat I stuck four red roses, that I might sooner by this token be taken notice of among the throng. For food I took bread, salt, and water, which by the counsel of an understanding person, I had at certain times used, not without profit, in the like occurrences. Before I parted from my cottage I first in this dress and wedding garment, fell down on my knees and besought God, that in case such a thing were, he would vouch-safe me a good issue. And thereupon in the presence of God I made a vow, that if anything through his grace should be revealed unto me, I would employ it neither to my own honour nor autho-rity in the world, but to the spreading of his name, and the ser-vices of my neighbour. And with this vow and good hope, I de-parted out of my cell with joy.

The Second Day.

I was hardly got outside of my Cell into a Forest, when me-thought that the whole heavens had already trimmed themselves against this wedding, for even the birds in my opinion chanted more pleasantly than before, and the young fawns skipped so merrily that they rejoiced my old heart, and moved me to sing. At length I espied a curious green heath, whither I betook myself out of the forest. Upon the heath stood three tall Cedars, to one of which was fastened a tablet, upon which was curious writing, offering to him who had heard anything concerning the nuptials of the king, four ways, all of which would lead to the royal court. The reader was exhorted to choose which he would, and to persevere therein, receiving at the same time warning as to the dangers to which he would be committed. As soon as I had read this writ-ing, all my joy was near vanished again, and I, who before sang merrily, began now inwardly to lament, for although I saw all the three ways before me, and understood that henceforward it was vouchsafed me to make choice of one of them; yet it troubled me that in case I went the stormy and rocky way, I might get a miser-able and deadly fall; or taking the long one, I might wander out of it through byways, or be otherwise detained in the great jour-ney. Neither durst I hope that I should be the very he, who should choose the royal way. I saw likewise the fourth before me, but it was so invironed with fire and exhalations, that I durst not draw near it, and therefore again and again considered whether I should return back, or take any of the ways before me. I presently drew out my bread and cut a slice of it, which a snow white dove, of whom I was not aware, sitting upon the tree, espyed and thereupon came down and betook herself very familiarly to me, to whom I willingly imparted my food, which she received, and so with her prettiness did again a little refresh me. But as soon as her enemy, a black raven, perceived it, he straight darted himself down upon the dove, and taking no notice of me, would needs force away the dove's meat, who could no otherwise guard herself but by flight; whereupon they both together flew towards the south, at which I was so hugely incensed and grieved, that without thinking what I did, I made haste after the filthy raven and so against my will ran into one of the forementioned ways a whole field's length, and thus the raven being chased away, and the dove delivered, I then first observed what I had inconsiderately done, and that I was already entered into a way, from which under peril of great punishment I durst not retire, and though I had still wherewith in some measure to comfort myself, yet that which was worst of all to me was, that I had left my bag and bread at the tree, and could never retrieve them again. At length upon a high hill afar off I espied a stately portal, to which not regarding how far it was distant, I hasted, because the sun had already hid himself under the hills, and I could elsewhere espy no abiding place, and this verily I ascribe only to God, who might well have permitted me to go forward in this way, and with-held my eyes that so I might have gazed beside this gate, to which I now made mighty haste, and reached it by so much daylight, as to take a very competent view of it. Now it was an exceeding Royal beautiful portal. As soon as I was come under it there stepped forth one in a sky coloured habit, whom I in friendly manner saluted, which though he thankfully returned it, yet he instantly demanded of me my letter of invitation. O how glad was I that I had then brought it with me. I quickly presented it, wherewith he was not only satisfied, but showed me abundance of respect, saying, come in, my brother, an acceptable guest you are to me ; and withall intreated me not to with-hold my name from him. Now having replied that I was a brother of the Red-Rosie Cross, he both wondered and seemed to rejoice at it, and then proceeded thus, My brother, have you nothing about you wherewith to purchase a token? I answered my ability was small, but if he saw anything about me he had a mind to, it was at his service. Now he having requested of me my bottle of water, and I granted it, he gives me a golden token, whereon stood no more but these two letters, S. C., intreating me that when it stood me in good stead, I would remember him. After which I asked him, how many were got in before me, which he also told me, and lastly out of mere friendship, gave me a sealed letter to the second porter. Now having lingered some time with him, the night grew on, whereupon a great beacon upon the gate was immediately fired, that so if any were still upon the way, he might make haste thither. At length after sufficient information, and an advantageous instruction, I friendly departed from the first porter. On the way, though, I would gladly have known what was written in my letter, yet since I had no reason to mistrust the porter, I forbare my purpose, and so went on the way, until I came likewise to the second gate which although it was very like the other, yet was it adorned with images and mystic significations. Under this gate lay a terrible grim lion, chain'd, who as soon as he espied me, arose and made at me with great roaring: whereupon the second porter, who lay upon a stone of marble, awaked, and wished me not to be troubled or affrighted, and then drove back the lion, and having received the letter, which I with trembling reached him, he read it, and with very great respect, spoke thus to me; Now well-come in God's Name unto me the man who of long time I

I

would gladly have seen. Meanwhile he also drew out a token, and asked me whether I could purchase it. But I having no thing else but my salt, presented it to him, which he thankfully accepted. Upon this token again stood only two letters, namely, S. M. Being now just about to enter discourse with him, it began to ring in the Castle, whereupon the porter counselled me to run apace, or else all the pains and labour I had hitherto taken would serve to no purpose, for the lights above began all ready to be extinguished; whereupon I dispatched with such great haste that I heeded not the porter, in such anguish was I, and truly it was but necessary, for I could not run so fast but that the Virgin, after whom all the lights were put out, was at my heels, and I should never have found the way, had not she with her torch, afforded me some light. I was moreover constrained to enter the very next to her, and the gate was so suddenly clapped to, that a part of my coat was locked out, which I verily was forced to leave behind me, for neither I nor they who stood ready without and called at the gate could prevail with the porter to open it again, but he delivered the keys to the Virgin, who took them with her into the court. Under this gate I was again to give my name, which was this last time written down in a little vellum book, and immediately with the rest dispatched to the Lord Bridegroom. Here it was where I first received the true Guest-Token, which was somewhat less than the former, but yet much heavier; upon this stood three letters S. P. N. Besides this, a new pair of shoes were given me, for the floor of the castle was laid with pure shining marble; my old shoes I was to give way to one of the poor who sat in throngs under the gate. Two pages, with as many torches, then conducted me into a little room; there they willed me to sit down on a form, which I did, but they, sticking their torches in two holes in the pavement, departed, and left me thus alone. Soon after I heard a noise, but saw nothing, and it proved to be certain men who

stumbled in upon me ; but since I could see nothing I was fain to
suffer and attend what they would do with me, but presently per-
ceiving them to be barbers, I intreated them not to justle me so,
for I was content to do whatever they desired, whereupon they
quickly let me go, and so one of them fine and gently cut away
the hair round about from the crown of my head, but on my
forehead, ears, and eyes, he permitted my grey locks to hang.

In this first encounter I was ready to despair, for inasmuch as
some of them shoved me so forcibly, and I could yet see nothing
I could think no other but that God, for my curiosity, had suffered
me to miscarry. Now these invisible barbers carefully gathered
up the hair which was cut off and carried it away with them.
After which the two pages entered again, and heartily laughed at
me for being so terrified. But they had scarcely spoken a few
words with me when again a little bell began to ring, which was
to give notice for assembling, whereupon they willed me rise, and
through many walks, doors, and winding stairs lighted me into a
spacious hall. In this room was a great multitude of guests,
emperors, kings, princes, and lords, noble and ignoble, rich and
poor, and all sorts of people, at which I hugely marvelled,
and thought to myself, ah, how gross a fool hast thou been to
engage upon this journey with so much bitterness and toil, when
here are even those fellows whom thou well knowest, and yet
had'st never any reason to esteem. They are now all here, and
thou with all thy prayers and supplications art hardly got in at
last. This, and more, the devil at that time injected, whom I
notwithstanding (as well as I could) directed to the issue. Mean-
time one or other of my acquaintance here and there spake to me :
Oh Brother Rosencreutz ! art thou here too ? Yea, my brethren, .
replied I; the grace of God hath helped me in also ; at which they
raised a mighty laughter, looking upon it as ridiculous that there
should be need of God in so slight an occasion. Now having

demanded each of them concerning his way, and found that most were forced to clamber over the rocks, certain trumpets (none of which we saw) began to sound to the table, whereupon they all seated themselves, everyone as he judged himself above the rest, so that for me and some other sorry fellows there was hardly a little nook left at the lower-most table.   Presently the two pages entered, and one of them said grace; after this meat was brought in, and albeit none could be seen, yet everything was so orderly managed, that it seemed to me as if every guest had had his proper attendant.   Now my artists having somewhat recruited themselves, and the wine having a little removed shame from their hearts, they presently began to vaunt and brag of their abilities. One would prove this, another that, and commonly the most sorry idiots made the loudest noise.   Ah, when I call to mind what preternatural and impossible enterprises I then heard, I am still ready to vomit at it.   In fine they never kept in their order, but whenever one rascal here, another there, could insinuate himself in between the nobles; then pretended they the finishing of such adventures as neither Sampson nor yet Hercules with all their strength could ever have achieved.   This would discharge Atlas of his burden; the other would again draw forth the three-headed Cerberus out of Hell.   In brief, every man had his own prate, and yet the great lords were so simple that they believed their pretences, and the rogues so audacious, that although one or other of them was here and there rapped over the fingers with a knife, yet they flinched not at it, but when any one perchance had filched a gold chain, then would all hazard for the like.   I saw one who heard the rustling of the heavens.   The second could see Plato's ideas.   A third could number Democritus's atoms.   There were also not a few pretenders to perpetual motion.   Many an one (in my opinion) had good understanding, but assumed too much to himself, to his own destruction.   Lastly, there was one also who would needs out of hand persuade us that he saw the servitors who attended, and would still have pursued his contention, had not one of those invisible waiters reached him so handsome a cuff upon his lying muzzle, that not only he, but many who were by him became as mute as mice. But it best of all pleased me, that all those, of whom I had any esteem were very quiet in their business, and made no loud cry of it, but acknowledged themselves to be *misunderstanding* men, to whom the mysteries of nature were too high, and they themselves much too small. In this tumult I had almost cursed the day wherein I came hither, for I could not but with anguish behold that those lewd vain people were above at the board, but I in so sorry a place could not, however, rest in peace, one of those rascals scornfully reproaching me for a motley fool. Now I thought not that there was yet one gate behind, through which we must pass, but imagined I was during the whole wedding, to continue in this scorn, contempt and indignity, which yet I had at no time deserved, either of the Lord Bridegroom or the Bride, and therefore (in my opinion) he should have done well to have sought out some other fool to his wedding than me. Behold, to such impatience doth the iniquity of this world reduce simple hearts. But this really was one part of my lameness, whereof I dreamed. And truly this clamour the longer it lasted, the more it increased. For there were already those who boasted of false and imaginary visions, and would persuade us of palpably lying dreams. Now there sat by me a very fine quiet man, who oftentimes discoursed of excellent matters, at length he said, Behold, my brother, if any one should now come who were willing to instruct these blockish people in the right way, would he be heard? No, verily, replied I. The world, said he, is now resolved (whatever comes on it) to be cheated, and cannot abide to give ear to those who intend its good. Seest thou also that same coxcomb, with what whimsical

figures and foolish conceits he allures others to him.   There, one
makes mouths at the people with unheard of mysterious words.
Yet believe me in this, the time is now coming when those shame-
ful Vizards shall be plucked off, and all the world shall know what
vagabond impostors were concealed behind them.   Then perhaps
that will be valued which at present is not esteemed.   Then there
began in the hall such excellent and stately music as all the days
of my life I never heard the like of.   After half an hour this
music ceased.   Presently after began a great noise of kettle drums,
trumpets, etc.   The door opened of itself and many thousand
small tapers came into the hall, all which of themselves marched
in so very exact order as altogether amazed us, till at last the two
fore-mentioned pages with bright torches, lighting in a most
beautiful virgin, all drawn on a gloriously gilded triumphant self-
moving throne, entered the hall.   It seemed to me she was the
very same who before on the way kindled and put out the lights,
and that these her attendants were the very same whom she
formerly placed at the trees.   She was not now as before in sky
colour, but arrayed in a snow white glittering robe which sparkled
of pure gold and cast such a lustre that we durst not steadily
behold it.

Such guests as chose to stay throughout the night, having an-
nounced their intention of so doing, were bound in their chambers
with cords, in such a way that they could by no means free themselves.   At length in my sorrowful thoughts I fell asleep.

The Third Day.

On the morrow all being assembled, the Trumpets, etc., began
again to sound and we imagined that the Bridegroom was ready
to present himself, which nevertheless was a huge mistake.   For
it was again the yesterday's Virgin who had arrayed herself all in
red velvet and girded herself with a white scarf.   Her train was

now no more of small tapers, but consisted of two hundred men in
harness who were all clothed in red and white. As soon as they
were alighted from the throne, she comes straight to us prisoners,
and after she had saluted us, she said in a few words : That some
of you have been sensible of your wretched condition is hugely
pleasing to my most mighty lord, and he is also resolved you shall
are the better for it. And having espied me in my habit, she
laughed and spake, good lack! Hast thou also submitted thyself
to the yoke? I imagined thou would'st have made thyself very
snug, which words caused my eyes to run over. After which she
commanded we should be unbound, and coupled together and
placed in a station where we might behold the scales, for, said
she, it may yet fare better with them than with the presumptuous
who yet stand here at liberty. Meanwhile the scales which were
entirely of gold were hung up in the midst of the hall. There
was also a little table covered with red velvet, and seven weights
placed thereon. First of all stood a pretty great one, next four
little ones, lastly, two great ones severally ; and these weights in
proportion to their bulk were so heavy that no man can believe or
comprehend it. The Virgin having sprung up into her high
throne, one of the pages commanded each one to place himself
according to his order, and one after the other, step into the
scales. One of the emperors made no scruple of it, but first of all
bowed himself a little towards the Virgin, and afterwards in all
his stately attire went up, whereupon each captain laid in his
weight, which (to the wonder of all) he stood out. But the last
was too heavy for him, so that forth he must, and that with such
anguish that the Virgin herself had pity on him, yet was the good
emperor bound and delivered over to the sixth band. Next came
forth another emperor, who stepped haughtily into the scale and
having a great thick book under his gown, he imagined not to
fail ; but being scarce able to abide the third weight, and being

unmercifully slung down, and his book in that affrightment
slipping from him, all the soldiers began to laugh, and he was
delivered up bound to the third band. Thus it went with some
others of the emperors. After these came forth a little short man
with a curled beard, an emperor too, who after the usual reverence
got up also, and held out so steadfastly, that methought had there
been more weights ready, he would have outstood them; to whom
the Virgin immediately arose, and bowed before him, causing him
to put on a gown of red velvet, and at last reached him a branch
of laurel, having good store of them upon her throne, upon the
steps whereof she willed him to sit down. After him, how it
fared with the rest of the emperors, kings and lords would be too
long to recount, but I cannot leave unmentioned that few of those
great personages held out. After the inquisition had also passed
over the gentry, the learned, and unlearned, and the rest, and in
each condition perhaps one, it may be, two, but for the most part
none, was found perfect, it came at length to those honest gentle-
men the vagabond cheaters, and rascally Lapidem Spitalanficum,
who were set upon the scale with such scorn that I myself for all
my grief was ready to burst with laughing, neither could the very
prisoners themselves refrain, for the most part could not abide
that severe trial, but with whips and scourges were jerked out of
the scale, and led to the other prisoners. Thus of so great a
throng so few remained, that I am ashamed to discover their
number.

The Inquisition being completely finished, and none but we
poor coupled hounds standing aside, at length one of the captains
stepped forth and said, Gracious Madam, if it please your lady-
ship, let these poor men who acknowledged their misunderstanding be set upon the scale, also without their incurring any danger
of penalty, and only for recreation's sake, if perchance anything
that is right may be found amongst them. We being untied

were one after another set up. My companion was the fifth who held out bravely, whereupon all, but especially the captain, applauded him, and the Virgin shewed him the usual respect. I was the eighth. Now as soon as (with trembling) I stepped up, my companion who already sat by in his velvet, looked friendly upon me, and the Virgin herself smiled a little. But for as much as I outstayed all the weights, the Virgin commanded them to draw me up by force, wherefore three men moreover hung on the other side of the beam, and yet could nothing prevail. Whereupon one of the pages immediately stood up and cried out exceeding loud, THAT'S HE, upon which the other replied, then let him gain his liberty, which the Virgin acceded, and being received with due ceremonies, the choice was given me to release one of the captives, whosoever I pleased. Afterwards a Council of the seven captains and us was set, and the business was propounded by the Virgin as president, who desired each one to give his opinion, how the prisoners were to be dealt with.

The story is a long one, and we must present the rest only in outline. It goes on to say that the kinds of punishment to be dealt out to the prisoners were then discussed and arranged, after which another banquet took place, when these captives were required to make confession of being cheats and vagabonds, which after some expostulation they agreed to, appealing at the same time for mercy which was refused, though variations in the degrees of punishment were promised.

When the sentences had all been executed, there came forward "a beautiful snow white Unicorn with a golden collar about his neck. In the same place he bowed himself down upon both his fore feet, as if hereby he had shewn honour to the Lyon, who stood so immoveably upon the fountain, that I took him to be of stone or brass, who immediately took the naked sword, which he

hare in his Paw and break it in the middle in two, the pieces
whereof to my thinking sunk into the fountain, after which he so
long roared, until a white dove brought a branch of olive in her
bill, which the Lyon devoured in an instant, and so was quieted.
And so the Unicorn returned to his place with joy, while our
Virgin led us down by the winding stairs."

The narrative grows complicated as it proceeds, and none the
less strange in its character; its details are inexplicable and
tedious, and it will be impossible to lay them before our readers.
The writer proceeds to describe his rambles about the castle, the
wonders which there met his gaze, his respectful treatment at the
banquet, and a problem proposed by the Virgin which was duly
debated by each in turn.

Fourth Day.

Presented to the King by the Virgin -who explained that the
lords had ventured hither with peril of body and life— assured by
Atlas of the King's welcome—promised by the Virgin that she
would remove the burden of his old age—performance of a comedy.

Fifth Day.

Further explorations of the castle—discovery of the burial place
of Lady Venus, "that beauty which hath undone many a great
man both in fortune, honour, blessing, and prosperity." Journey
with the Virgin to the Tower of Olympus.

Sixth Day.

Distribution by lot of Ladders, Ropes and Wings—the mysterious bird—restoring the dead to life.

Seventh Day.

"After eight o'clock I awaked and quickly made myself ready,
being desirous to return again into the tower, but the dark
passages in the wall were so many and various that I wandered a

good while before I could find the way out. The same happened
to the rest, too, till at last we all met again in the neathermost
vault, and habits entirely yellow were given us, together with our
golden fleeces. At that time the Virgin declared to us that we
were Knights of the Golden Stone, of which we were before ignorant. After we had now thus made ourselves ready and taken
our breakfasts, the old man presented each of us with a medal of
gold; on the one side stood these words: AR. NAT. MI. On
the other these, TEM. NA. F.

Exhorting us, moreover, we should enterprise nothing beyond
and against this token of remembrance. Herewith we went to
the sea, where our ships lay so richly equipped, that it was not
well possible but that such brave things must first have been
brought thither. The ships were twelve in number; our flags
were the twelve celestial signs, and we sate in Libra. Besides
other things, our ship had also a noble and curious clock, which
shewed us all the minutes. The ships passed on and before we
had sailed two hours the mariner told us that he already saw the
whole lake almost covered with ships, by which we could conjec-
ture they were come but to meet us, which also proved true. As
soon as they were well in ken of us, the pieces were discharged
on both sides, and there was such a din of trumpets, shalms, and
kettledrums that all the ships upon the sea capered again. Finally
as soon as we came near they brought our ships together and so
made a stand. Immediately the old Atlas stepped forth on the
King's behalf, making a short but handsome oration, wherein he
welcomed us and demanded whether the royal presents were in
readiness. The rest of my companions were in an huge amaze-
ment, whence this king should arise, for they imagined no other
but that they must again awaken him. We suffered them to
continue in their wonderment, and carried ourselves as if it seemed
strange to us too. After Atlas's oration, out steps our old man

making somewhat a larger reply, wherein he wished the King and Queen all happiness and increase, after which he delivered up a curious small casket, but what was in it I know not; only it was committed to Cupid, who hovered between them both, to keep. After the oration was finished, they again let off a joyful volley of shot, and so we sailed on a good time together, till at length we arrived at another shore. This was near the first gate at which I first entered. At this place again there attended a great multitude of the King's family together with some hundreds of horses. Our old lord and I most unworthy were to ride even with the King, each of us bearing a snow white ensign, with a red cross. I had fastened my tokens round my hat of which the young King soon took notice, and demanded if I were he, who could at the gate redeem those tokens? I answered in the most humble manner, Yes. But he laughed on me, saying, there henceforth needed no ceremony; I was his father. Then he asked wherewith I had redeemed them. I replied, with water and salt, whereupon he wondered who had made me so wise, upon which I grew somewhat more confident, and recounted unto him, how it had happened to me with my bread, the dove, and the raven, and he was pleased with it, and said expressly that it must needs be that God had herein vouchsafed me a singular happiness............Meantime the tables were prepared in a spacious room, in which we had never been before; into this we were conducted with singular pomp and ceremony. This was the last noblest meal at which I was present. After the banquet the tables were suddenly taken away, and certain curious chairs placed round about in circle, in which we together with the King and Queen, both their old men, the ladies and virgins were to sit. After which a very handsome page opened the above mentioned glorious little book, when Atlas immediately placing himself in the midst, began to bespeak us to the ensuing purpose. That his royal majesty had not yet committed to oblivion the service we had done, and how carefully we had attended our duty, and therefore by way of retribution had elected all and each of us Knights of the Golden Stone. That it was therefore further necessary not only once again to oblige ourselves towards his royal majesty, but to now swear too upon the following articles, and then his royal majesty would likewise know how to behave himself towards his liege people. Upon which he caused the page to read over the articles, which were these :—

1.—You my lords the knights, shall swear, that you shall at no time ascribe your order either unto any devil, or spirit, but only to God your Creator, and his handmaid Nature.

2.—That you will abominate all whoredom, incontinency and uncleanness, and not defile your order with such vices.

3.—That you through your talents will be ready to assist all that are worthy, and have need of them.

4.—That you desire not to employ this honour to worldly pride and high authority.

5.—That you shall not be willing to live longer than God will have you.

Now being to vow to them all by the King's sceptre, we were afterwards with the usual ceremonies installed knights, and amongst other privileges set our ignorance, poverty and sickness ; to handle them at our pleasure. And this was afterwards ratified in a little chapel, and thanks returned to God for it. And because every one was there to write his name, I writ thus,

Summa Scientia nihil Scire,

Fr. Christianus Rosencreutz,

Eques aurei Lapidis,

Anno 1549."

CPSIA information can be obtained at www.ICGtesting.com
262089BV00010BA/76/P